DO WHAT YOU LIKE

JOBS IF YOU LIKE
the Arts

Terri Dougherty

San Diego, CA

About the Author

Terri Dougherty has written more than one hundred books for children and young adults. She loves exploring new areas and has written about a variety of topics. She lives in Appleton, Wisconsin, with her husband, Denis. They enjoy hiking, biking, and traveling, especially visiting their three grown children.

© 2025 ReferencePoint Press, Inc.
Printed in the United States

For more information, contact:
ReferencePoint Press, Inc.
PO Box 27779
San Diego, CA 92198
www.ReferencePointPress.com

ALL RIGHTS RESERVED.
No part of this work covered by the copyright hereon may be reproduced or used in any form or by any means—graphic, electronic, or mechanical, including photocopying, recording, taping, web distribution, or information storage retrieval systems—without the written permission of the publisher.

Picture Credits:
Cover: YAKOBCHUK VIACHESLAV/Shutterstock
10: REDPIXEL/Shutterstock
19: Money Business Images/Shutterstock
26: Jacob Kund/Shutterstock
35: PeopleImages.com-Yuri A/Shutterstock
42: Peakstock/Shutterstock

LIBRARY OF CONGRESS CATALOGING-IN-PUBLICATION DATA

Names: Dougherty, Terri, author.
Title: Jobs if you like the arts / by Terri Dougherty.
Description: San Diego, CA : ReferencePoint Press, Inc., 2025. | Series: Do what you like | Includes bibliographical references and index.
Identifiers: LCCN 2024035119 (print) | LCCN 2024035120 (ebook) | ISBN 9781678209803 (library binding) | ISBN 9781678209810 (ebook)
Subjects: LCSH: Cultural industries--Vocational guidance--Juvenile literature. | Arts--Vocational guidance--Juvenile literature.
Classification: LCC HD9999.C9472 D68 2025 (print) | LCC HD9999.C9472 (ebook) | DDC 700.23--dc23/eng/20240926
LC record available at https://lccn.loc.gov/2024035119
LC ebook record available at https://lccn.loc.gov/2024035120

Contents

Introduction: Where Can an Interest in the Arts Take You?	4
Graphic Designer	7
Art Teacher	15
Craft or Fine Artist	23
Dancer	31
Art Therapist	39
Sound Engineering Technician	47
Source Notes	55
Interview with a Craft Artist	58
Other Jobs If You Like the Arts	61
Index	62

Introduction: Where Can an Interest in the Arts Take You?

Drawing, dancing, or singing might be your passion. Maybe you cannot wait to get onstage for your next performance or head to the garage with your bandmates for a jam session. Your perfect day might be to take an easel and paintbrush outside and transform a canvas into the scene in front of you.

Can your passion for the arts translate into a career? Absolutely. Just as there are countless ways to turn notes into a song or colors into a picture, there are a variety of ways to turn a love of art, music, or theater into a fulfilling and fascinating career. Damien Harris's interest in music began when he was a trombone player in the high school jazz band. This has led to work as an audio engineer and production manager for a jazz artist. He has also worked in a recording studio and with a touring group as a production manager and mixer. "I was always into things and wanted to know how things worked," he says. "I always tried to learn more."[1]

Opportunities for a career in the arts might be more varied than you would expect. Becoming a superstar singer or Oscar-winning actor can certainly be a goal, but that is far from the only way to be successful. Arts professionals work as teachers, choreographers, composers, sound technicians, designers, directors, and in many other occupations that allow their creativity and talent to shine. Joseph Ferlo is the director of a local arts center in Wisconsin that is more than 140 years old. During his career he has been a piano accompanist, local musical producer, and the director of three other historic theaters. His work supports his interest in the arts and makes a positive community impact.

In addition to providing the opportunity to work for interesting organizations, such as a performing arts center or recording studio, a job in the arts can offer the opportunity for independence. Some people with jobs in the arts pursue their interest through part-time work or self-employment. A singer or musician might perform on weekends and have another job during the week. A piano, guitar, or voice teacher might instruct students at his or her own studio.

A career in the arts is not without challenges. Some jobs with high salaries, such as a role in a play or television series, are extremely competitive. Part-time work may not come with benefits. Employment could be seasonal rather than year round. A job could end when a movie wraps up production, a play closes, or a concert tour makes its final stop. Those working in the arts may find that they are often looking for new work opportunities and need to network with others in the field to learn about job openings.

There are jobs that use artistic talent that are steady and good-paying, however. The median annual pay for art directors is $106,500, the Bureau of Labor Statistics (BLS) notes. Industrial designers—who combine art, business, and engineering skills—earn a median salary of $76,250 each year. BLS statistics also show that the median annual wage for people working in arts and design occupations is $51,660, higher than the median annual wage of $48,060 for all occupations.

Artistic job opportunities are expected to keep pace with average job growth for all occupations. According to the BLS, from 2022 to 2032,

- an average of 95,800 job openings are expected each year in arts and design occupations,
- about 9,300 job openings are expected each year for actors,
- around 22,600 job openings for musicians and singers are expected each year, and
- about 3,000 job openings for dancers and choreographers are expected each year.

A job in the arts can be rewarding and fulfilling, and training toward a career in the arts helps develop qualities that are valuable in any occupation. Dedication, perseverance, and hard work are required to develop an artistic gift or talent. These skills can help you conquer challenges and overcome obstacles. Pursuing an occupation that builds on your interest in the arts can reward you with a career path that is interesting, exciting, and fulfilling.

Graphic Designer

What Does a Graphic Designer Do?

Tessa Hansen's graphics show the pride and grit of the Charlotte Football Club. Her images featuring team celebrations and game faces of the professional soccer team are on billboards, banners, and social media. "Going into every project I'm trying to think of what people want to see, like your favorite player on match day or the story behind their latest milestone,"[2] she says.

Freelance graphic designer Jesse Nyberg creates movie posters, print ads, and social media graphics for clients. His creations emphasize type styles and texture, and much of his work reflects an interest in music. He also creates and edits YouTube videos and puts out a newsletter focusing on graphic design.

Graphic designers like Hansen and Nyberg use text and images to convey concepts and ideas. Their work can motivate a team's fans, capture a brand's identity, or illustrate an article's meaning. They use creativity, artistic ability, and technical skill to create original designs that inform and inspire their audience. Their work can be found on packages and posters, as well as in advertisements, magazines, and company reports. Graphic designers are called on to make images

A Few Facts

Typical Earnings
Median annual pay of $58,910 in 2023

Educational Requirements
Bachelor's degree

Personal Qualities
Artistic ability, analytical skills, communication skills, computer skills, creativity, time management

Work Settings
Office or studio

Future Outlook
Growth rate of 3 percent through 2032

and logos that are visually appealing, but they must do more than catch the eye. "We need to solve problems, tell stories, and create meaningful connections between brands and their audience,"[3] says Eddie Deva, creative director at PixelBull.

The assortment of work available to graphic artists appeals to Amy Lewin. Lewin loves variety in design and enjoys changing her style. During her career she has helped small businesses create their brand, produced print pieces for pharmaceutical companies, and made online and retail marketing advertisements. She has also been a senior graphic designer at a video game publishing company, where she created package designs for video games and worked as the art director for a commercial. "As an undergrad, I never would have imagined my trajectory would provide me with so many opportunities,"[4] she says.

The Workday

At 9:00 a.m., Nyberg positions himself in front of the computer keyboard and monitors in his home office. He starts the day by working on the design for a client's movie poster. "The reason I try to do the most important work early in the day is to make sure I'm using my best energy on what matters most," he says. Later in the day he takes on tasks he finds more relaxing. He researches design ideas by looking through books containing images of book and record album covers. He catalogs his favorites on his computer to use as inspiration for future projects. In addition, he edits videos that are posted on YouTube. "Editing is a nice change of pace from concept-heavy design stuff,"[5] he says.

Graphic designer Dimpho Baguley specializes in branding for her clients. Her projects for the day can include creating business cards, editing video footage, and creating social media posts. She also takes care of the business side of her company, Vona Studios, which means she needs to update the website, post on social media, and send out invoices. A graphic designer's sched-

> **Find Your Niche Even If You Are Not an Artist**
>
> "You don't have to be an artist to be a graphic designer. I used to always think I had to be good at all aspects of art to be a graphic designer. In reality, it's such a broad field that anyone can find their niche within it. Just because I don't know my way around a paintbrush, doesn't mean I can't design a slick website. Try a bit of everything until you discover what you're best at."
>
> —Kieren Colquitt, lead graphic designer at Sood Marketing
>
> Quoted in Brianna Flavin, "Is Graphic Design a Good Career? What I Wish I Knew BEFORE Becoming a Graphic Designer," *Design Blog*, Rasmussen University, May 19, 2023. www.rasmussen.edu.

ule is often driven by project deadlines, and Baguley sometimes works on the weekend to capture video footage for a client or edit and post videos.

Graphic designers who work in an office often spend part of their day collaborating with team members as well as clients, writers, and others. "I used to think that designers work alone," Deva says. "As I worked with larger companies, I learned that designers, developers, and the marketing team need to collaborate closely. It was surprising but also exciting to see how much can be achieved through teamwork."[6]

Education and Training

Graphic designers usually need a bachelor's degree in graphic design, or they might have a degree in another field and have graphic design training. Technical skills in design, as well as project management and business skills, are part of a graphic designer's education. Classes can include design theory, digital media, digital effects, motion graphics, and animation. Courses in studio art, website design, typography, printing techniques, commercial graphics production, and 3-D modeling may also be part

A graphic designer works on various logo ideas for a new client. Graphic designers use text, images, fonts, colors, and lines to convey concepts and ideas that will attract customers and strengthen their connection to the brand.

of the curriculum. Students often build a portfolio that showcases their work.

The digital side of graphic design can be especially important when looking for a job. Gabe Ruane, cofounder of Turn Agency, found that having animation skills made him more marketable. "Everything happens on screens,"[7] Ruane says.

Skills and Personality

Graphic designers need to be artistic and creative because they are typically required to find innovative ways to present complex ideas and information. They must also be analytic, strategic, and practical and need good problem-solving skills because the message they convey needs to be clear and easily understood. "Good design goes beyond just aesthetics and plays a crucial role in creating a visual language that communicates information and ideas in a clear, concise, visually-engaging way in order to achieve specific goals,"[8] explains Alysia Steingart, visual identity designer at Grove Brands.

When working with clients, graphic designers sometimes need to put their egos aside. The final design might not be what the graphic designer prefers, but it could be what the client wants. When it comes to the final product, the client's decision prevails. Graphic designers need to take a practical approach to their work and balance their artistic side with the client's requirements.

Because their job is to convey information, communication skills are essential for graphic designers. In addition to sharing ideas through their work, they help clients, associates, and managers understand what goes into the piece they are creating and the amount of effort it will take to get it from a concept to a finished product. "When clients ask for seemingly small adjustments, it likely isn't something you can fix in just a few minutes," says Anna Bacon, graphic design specialist at Adduco Communications. "Design takes a lot of time and care, and sometimes you'll have to explain this to an impatient client more than once."[9]

Another important skill for graphic artists is time management. They may be working on several projects at the same time, and each will have its own timetable. They need to know how to properly allocate their time so everything gets done by the deadline.

Work Settings

Graphic designers often work in a studio or office setting. Many use computers loaded with design software. They may also work at a drafting table while creating physical pieces of art that then may be scanned into the computer and used in a project.

Those who have their own business often work independently from their home, while those in an office are commonly part of a design team. As part of the creative team for the Charlotte Football Club, Hansen works with a photographer, a video coordinator, and another senior graphic designer. She finds her coworkers to be a valuable source of job-related knowledge. "They were able to teach me a lot of the technical things going into it and provide that support that I didn't think that I needed,"[10] she notes.

Employers and Earnings

Graphic designers often work for advertising or public relations firms or companies that offer graphic design services. They may also work for publishers and printers. About a fifth of graphic designers are self-employed. In addition to doing graphic design, they dedicate time to running their business—for example, billing current clients and promoting their services to find new ones.

A graphic designer may take on additional responsibilities and move into a position as an art director or creative director. In addition to creating designs, an art director leads a team of designers and other creative professionals. The art director may oversee the visual style of a magazine, product, or video production. A creative director works for an advertising agency, marketing firm, or another business to lead a team of professionals who develop a creative strategy and vision for clients. Directors make sure a project stays within budget, has the right impact, and has a consistent style.

A graphic designer may also gravitate to a web design role. User interface (UI) and user experience (UX) designers use web technology as well as graphic design skills. A UX designer makes sure a website has an appealing style and is easy to navigate. A UI designer works with the elements on a web page or screen, making sure the style is consistent with the site's overall design.

The median pay for graphic designers was $58,910 in May 2023, according to the Bureau of Labor Statistics. Half of graphic designers made more than this amount, and half made less.

Fulfilling Experience

"With two architects for parents, I've always been interested in the interdisciplinary work that occurs between graphic design and architecture, and I had a feeling EGD [experiential graphic design] would be the perfect niche for me. [As a co-op student at the Society for Experiential Graphic Design (SEGD)], I designed a timeline to represent SEGD history starting in 1973 when SEGD was founded. It was extremely rewarding to see my timeline in person at the [SEGD 50th] conference and watch attendees interact with it, sometimes even finding an event they took part in or their own name."

—Hannah LoGalbo, design student

Hannah LoGalbo, "SEGD Love Stories—Hannah LoGalbo," SEGD, May 22, 2024. www.segd.org.

Those offering specialized design services had the highest annual median wage of $62,330.

Future Outlook

The Bureau of Labor Statistics (BLS) projects job growth of 3 percent through 2032 for graphic designers, which is as fast as average for jobs overall. The need for social media site designers will support job growth, although the bureau expects a decline in demand for designers who work for print magazines and newspapers. The BLS anticipates 22,800 job openings each year for graphic designers.

Those looking to use a background in graphic design to move into other roles may find additional opportunities. Jobs for web and digital interface designers are expected to grow by 15 percent by 2032, with 16,700 job openings each year. Art director jobs are expected to grow at 6 percent, and the BLS anticipates 13,800 job openings annually for art directors.

Find Out More

American Institute of Graphic Arts (AIGA)
www.aiga.org

The website for AIGA, a professional association for designers, offers information about working in design, news about the industry, and networking opportunities. The Student section provides information about internships, professional standards, and design careers. Podcasts and articles focus on issues of interest to designers.

Graphic Artists Guild
www.graphicartistsguild.org

The Graphic Artists Guild website provides resources for graphic artists. It has reviews of graphic novels and articles about issues graphic artists face, such as copyright infringement. Its webinars, which nonmembers can view for a fee, examine trends and feature interviews with those working in the field.

Society for Experiential Graphic Design (SEGD)
www.segd.org

The SEGD supports designers who work with elements of design that make human environments engaging, inclusive, and easy to navigate. Its members include designers, architects, and media developers, and its website looks at the contributions that designers make to living communities. The Resources and Education section features articles on people who work in design.

Art Teacher

What Does an Art Teacher Do?

Art teacher Kristina Brown needs to be creative, inventive, and organized each day, since she uses a broad range of artistic techniques and materials with her students. In the morning she might teach about pinhole photography, and in the afternoon she could focus on blending poetry and art. She also needs to keep art supplies organized and navigate logistical challenges such as finding places for student artwork to dry. "The spectrum of what we teach daily is unmatched," Brown says. "We understand the importance of establishing routines to ensure creative chaos doesn't turn into a complete mess. While outsiders may see harmony and creativity flowing in our classroom, we know it takes a lot of trial and error and finesse!"[11]

Paper chains are a favorite project for Ishel Hertz's elementary school students, and they love competing to try to make the longest one. She collects them at the end of class by having students hang them over her arms and shoulders; soon she is covered with them. A day's projects can also include creating paper flowers and clay sunflowers,

---

A Few Facts

Typical Earnings
Median annual pay in 2023, $63,680 for elementary school teachers; $65,220 for high school teachers

Educational Requirements
Bachelor's degree, teaching certification

Personal Qualities
Artistic ability, creativity, communication skills, patience, resourcefulness

Work Settings
Classroom

Future Outlook
Growth rate of 1 percent through 2032

Ultimately, a Rewarding Ride

"Being a teacher is a bit of an emotional roller coaster. Every school year has highs and lows. It has new challenges, unexpected twists and turns, and it's going to keep you on your toes. You've got to have a really good support system. You're going to need to vent about work. You're going to cry sometimes about work, you're going to laugh about work, you're going to get angry and frustrated about things that happen at school but you're going to love it. It's going to be a wonderful and rewarding career that you will enjoy."

—Katie Jarvis, elementary school art teacher

Katie Jarvis, *Want to Be an Art Teacher? 10 Realities You Must Know About*, YouTube, March 23, 2024. www.youtube.com/watch?v=qkTA516bIW4.

---

as well as coloring pictures of hot air balloons. For her, being an art teacher is the best job in the world.

Andrea Wlodarczyk sees teaching art as more than helping students learn how to paint and draw. "An art teacher's superpower is the ability to quickly tune into a student's inner world through their art," she says. "You can support them as they navigate their feelings. Some students find their anchor in your art class, which motivates them to work in other classes."[12]

Art teachers teach concepts such as color, form, and texture in elementary, middle school, and high school classes, and they introduce artistic styles and materials to their students. They follow a curriculum for each grade level, but they bring out students' imaginative sides as they help them express themselves creatively and share emotions and ideas through art.

The Workday

Elementary school art teacher Katie Vander Velden teaches up to six fifty-minute classes each day. Before school she sets up for the day and cuts paper, sharpens pencils, pours paint, or prepares other materials. Younger students typically do multiple hands-on activities during a class period, while older students focus on a more rigorous project. She explains:

> A typical class has instruction and demonstration time, work time, and clean up. At the beginning of a class I give a lesson and demonstration for the art project, and teach about any materials or artists the students are learning about. During work time, I walk around the room helping and checking in with students. At the end of class, the students and I clean up their projects and supplies.[13]

After a class period ends, she has about ten minutes to prepare for the next group of students to arrive.

A typical day involves three classes in the morning and three in the afternoon, or two afternoon classes and a prep period. "This schedule keeps you moving all day long,"[14] she says. After school, she washes tables, cleans paintbrushes, tidies up the room, and gets ready for the next day.

Students in every grade attend art class weekly, so by the end of the week Vander Velden has taught every student in the school. In addition to being adept at teaching students of diverse ages and skill levels, art teachers may also monitor students during lunch or recess and advise after-school clubs. Wlodarczyk takes part in a school-wide reading program, hosting students in her classroom four days a week. "Even though we are art teachers, we are still responsible team players," she says. "It is important that we do our part to make sure school programs are successful."[15]

Education and Training

Art teachers usually have a bachelor's degree in art education. A public school teacher needs a teaching certification or license from the state. College classes may include color theory, drawing, composition, digital media, 3-D design, and art history. Teaching skills such as classroom management, lesson planning, and curriculum development are also part of an art education program. To cap off their studies, aspiring art teachers do student teaching in an elementary, middle, or high school classroom under the guidance of an experienced teacher.

An art major may also get a teaching license after graduating from college. Vander Velden majored in art and took additional classes during her first year of teaching to get her license. "I started teaching summer school art classes on a bit of a whim and was put in touch with the school district's fine arts coordinator," she recalls. "She spoke about how I would be a great fit to be a full-time art teacher and the pieces just fell into place. I had never thought of being a teacher during my years in college, but, looking back, I think my love of learning and art made me become an art teacher."[16]

Skills and Personality

In addition to being creative and having artistic ability, art teachers must be organized and learn on the job. "There's no resource that just covers it all and tells you exactly what to do," teacher Katie Jarvis points out. "You might be one of the few art teachers that is there in your building. You also might be alone, so you're kind of figuring this out as you go."[17] Art teachers must figure out how to set up their room, order supplies, establish classroom routines, and create lesson plans. They need to develop projects for each class and keep students on track to complete them.

Art teachers also need the patience, confidence, and skills to deal with students who have trouble focusing or are disruptive. "Young students are often very excited to be in art class, which is awesome, but it can be hard to handle that level of energy all day every day," Vander Velden notes. Her least favorite part of be-

A high school art teacher assists students with their paintings. Art teachers work with students of all ages. They teach concepts such as color, form, and texture and encourage creative expression.

ing a teacher is dealing with discipline issues. "As a teacher, you encounter various bad behaviors on a daily basis."[18]

Working Conditions

Art teachers work in a classroom. They may work at a single school or travel to different schools during the week or the school day. Art teachers may have their own classroom that is dedicated to art or may travel from classroom to classroom with art supplies in tow. Vander Velden has worked in both settings. She says:

> In the past, I had a rolling cart of art supplies that I took to science classrooms for art class. This was a bit tough because it did not prioritize the creation of art or feel very

permanent. Now, within my art rooms, I am able to decorate, arrange, and organize the entire space to foster creativity. My art rooms are colorful, sometimes messy, noisy, and fun. I try to create a space that invites students to want to make art. My rooms have cabinets and drawers full of every art supply I can get my hands on.[19]

Teachers typically work during a ten-month school year and have two months off in the summer as well as weeklong winter and spring breaks. A district may also have a year-round schedule with each nine-week school session followed by a three-week break. "I love that I am able to have breaks throughout the year to dedicate to my own artistic practice,"[20] Vander Velden says.

During summer break, art teachers may teach summer school or attend classes themselves to continue their education. They may also spend time planning for the next school year.

Employers and Earnings

Art teachers work for public and private schools. The median (which means that half earned more, and half earned less) annual pay for elementary school teachers was $63,680 in 2023. The median annual pay for middle school teachers was $64,290, while high school teachers earned a median salary of $65,220 annually.

The highest-paid elementary school teachers earned more than $104,440, according to the Bureau of Labor Statistics (BLS), while the highest-paid middle school teachers earned $104,410. The highest-paid high school teachers earned more than $106,380. Some of this higher pay may be due to the standard of living in certain areas of the country; some might also come from assuming

> **A Balancing Act**
>
> "A day in the life of this art teacher is dedicated to the invisible parts of teaching—strategically thinking and planning through the day and beyond, arranging the space, organizing supplies, and communicating to and between all of our stakeholders. Although our paint-splattered hands are constantly balancing the administrative teacher and studio artist duties, we wouldn't have it any other way."
>
> —Andrea Wlodarczyk, former middle school art teacher
>
> Andrea Wlodarczyk, "What Does a Day in the Life of an Art Teacher Look Like?," The Art of Education University, April 22, 2022. www.theartofeducation.edu.

other duties within schools, such as coaching a team or taking on extra classes, like those that provide college credit to high school students.

Future Outlook

The Bureau of Labor Statistics (BLS) expects the overall number of teachers to grow by about 1 percent by 2032, which is lower than the average 3 percent growth for all occupations. This reflects a decline in the school-aged population since 2019. However, because there is still a need for teachers throughout the United States, the BLS projects that there will be thousands of job openings for kindergarten, elementary, and high school teachers in the coming years, and this includes art teachers.

The job openings are expected to occur due to teachers retiring or moving into different occupations. There are 109,000 job openings projected each year for kindergarten and elementary school teachers, 42,200 for middle school teachers, and 67,100 for high school teachers.

Find Out More

National Art Education Association

www.arteducators.org

News about art education trends, events, and resources is a feature of the website for the National Art Education Association, a professional membership organization for visual arts, design, and media arts teachers. The site's Opportunities section includes information about the Scholastic Art & Writing Awards for students in seventh to twelfth grade.

National Gallery of Art

www.nga.gov

The website for the National Gallery of Art in Washington, DC, has a section for teachers. It offers lesson plans for students from kindergarten age to the university level. Its resources include lessons that provide a deeper look at artists and art movements. It also offers online classes that link critical thinking skills to art.

Teach.org

www.teach.org

This site from the US Department of Education offers resources for individuals considering a career as a teacher. It gives an overview of the job, has articles and videos about teaching, and showcases career paths. It also has advice on how to choose a teaching program and earn a teaching license.

Craft or Fine Artist

What Does a Craft or Fine Artist Do?

Cedric Mitchell makes richly colored drinking glasses that double as funky, innovative works of art. The glasses created by the Los Angeles artist have a rounded bottom, making them tilt so a drink can be swiveled inside them. He also makes tumblers and vases in vibrant colors. "My studio art glass practice fuses pop art influences with postmodern innovation,"[21] he explains.

Woodworker Eric Meyer creates and sells calipers, hammers, and other tools that are carefully designed and decorated. The first tool he made was a small hammer, which he crafted from brass and maple. "The process proved so fun, I made a few more, with the simple goal of improving upon the last,"[22] he says.

While attending college, Ger Xiong fell in love with metalsmithing. He now works with metals, textiles, and jewelry and uses his work to document the history of the Hmong people, who fought on the side of the United States during the Vietnam War and were forced to leave their country and make a new life for themselves in the United States. "Documenting

A Few Facts

Typical Earnings
Median annual pay of $52,910 in 2023

Educational Requirements
No formal requirements, but a bachelor's degree is common

Personal Qualities
Artistic ability, creativity, business and customer service skills, communication and interpersonal skills

Work Settings
Studio

Future Outlook
Growth rate of 4 percent through 2032

our history through textiles and objects has provided ways to preserve my Hmong identity, culture, and history,"[23] he says.

Craft and fine artists create original items that are beautiful, meaningful, and often functional. Artists may make jewelry, pottery, furniture, clothing, stained glass, paintings, or sculptures. They use creativity, talent, and skill to create one-of-a-kind, handmade pieces. The items may be showcased in exhibits at museums or sold to the public at craft shows, in art galleries, or through an artist's online shop.

The Workday

Artists often set their own schedule, balancing their creative flow with the need to meet a deadline or fulfill an order. They may need to work long days or on weekends when filling an order. Fran Failla becomes immersed in her work when creating oil paintings, but she finds that breaks are essential. Her daily routine typically includes taking her dog for a walk and stopping at a local restaurant to eat. "When you're in front of a canvas for hours on end, your vision tends to not 'stretch' and you can get really tired, so it's a good idea to take walks, look around and keep a good balance of 'near and far' in your own personal world,"[24] she advises.

Abstract painter Jess Engle begins her workday by writing in a journal and browsing Pinterest for inspiration. She then sketches ideas in spiral notebooks. "Often what happens is that there are just these shapes that I'm kind of obsessed with that . . . will come through in the larger pieces of work that I do,"[25] she explains.

After breakfast she begins work on a new piece, stopping when she needs a break. "I know when that is because things just stop flowing and I start feeling like I'm kind of forcing my will onto a piece," she says. After a walk outdoors in a garden, she returns to the studio at 11:30 a.m. to work on another abstract piece. Her next task is to create a social media post about her work. "I usually share slices of life and bits of my day, especially

Artists See the World Differently

"An artist is a visionary. We are the creators of tomorrow and our imaginations broadly view life in a way that is unfathomable to others. Where others see a store, a street, a bus, or an office, an artist sees color and form and movement and Life. Therefore, I find for myself that after I've spent several days furiously painting, I'm exhausted, both emotionally and mentally. I need to take some time to breathe . . . to pull back and regroup. Then, once refreshed, I can plunge back into the immense joy of painting once again."

—Fran Failla, oil painter

Fran Failla, "A Day in the Life of an Artist," *Fran Failla Fine Art* (blog), February 22, 2023. www.franfailla.com.

the abstracts,"[26] she says. At 2:30 p.m. she has a sketching session, using colored pencils and pastels to create a sketch of a pomegranate. After placing the fruit sketch in the corner of her studio at 4:30 p.m., she edits a video file about her day that is posted on YouTube.

For some, being an artist is a part-time job. Nicole Tocci creates necklaces from vintage buttons, spending about twenty hours a week on her jewelry business. She creates social media posts for the business in the morning and evening and spends some Saturdays scouring vintage clothing shops for buttons to use in the creation of jewelry.

Education and Training

A formal degree is not needed to become a craft or fine artist, but most pursue training beyond high school. Xiong has a bachelor of fine arts degree, with an emphasis in metals and jewelry, and a master of fine arts degree. Engle has a bachelor's degree in fashion design and a master's degree in creative advertising.

A young ceramic artist uses a pottery wheel to craft a bowl or vase. Craft and fine artists create original items that are beautiful, meaningful, and often functional. They might work with jewelry, pottery, furniture, clothing, stained glass, paintings, sculptures, or other items.

In college, art students usually study art history and take classes related to their area of interest, such as painting, metalworking, or sculpting. They also take core classes in English, science, and social science. They may also take business-related classes such as marketing.

Student artists develop a portfolio of their work that showcases their talent and style. Employers assess the artist's portfolio when deciding whether he or she is a good fit for a job. Artists who have their own business show their portfolio to clients, who may buy their artwork or commission them to do a project.

Artists may also be self-taught or take classes that help them refine a skill or technique. Mitchell learned glassblowing at the

Tulsa Glassblowing School, for example. Award-winning ceramic artist and potter Kristina Batiste had no formal training until her thirties, when she became involved in pottery through a community college and local classes.

Skills and Personality

Craft and fine artists must be creative and have artistic skills. They need to make original artwork that others want to have because of its beauty, uniqueness, or look, and most hope to develop their own style that sets them apart from other artists. Since many fine arts and crafts require precision in handling tools—whether paintbrush, soldering iron, or potter's wheel—artists commonly have to be quite dexterous to make their vision come to life.

Fine and craft artists are often self-employed, selling as well as creating their artwork. Strong interpersonal skills are needed since they work with clients or gallery owners and others who showcase and sell their work. Business skills are also an asset since they set prices, work out contract terms, and keep track of what is being earned and spent. They also need to understand the market for their work and stay on top of trends and styles.

Like Engle, artists often market their pieces through social media posts and videos that showcase their work. They need to be skilled at content creation and posting, or they might hire someone to take on that task. Many artists also sell their works online and therefore need to maintain a website or pay to have someone else manage it.

Work Settings

Artists typically work in a studio located in their home, an office building, a warehouse, or a loft. They may share the studio space with other artists and exhibit their work there. Engle has a home studio, using the sunroom to work on her pieces and a front hall to hang works of art in progress. Meyer does woodworking in a small studio that includes a workbench, tools, and lumber.

Depending on the materials they are using, artists may need to be mindful of safety. They need to protect themselves from exposure to the chemicals that are in the paint, glue, ink, and other materials they use. Breathing masks and goggles need to be worn while they are working with certain materials, and caution is needed when using equipment such as a kiln.

Employers and Earnings

More than half of craft and fine artists are self-employed, and most work full time. Many craft and fine artists engage in other part-time work while building their business. Of those who are not self-employed, the Bureau of Labor Statistics (BLS) notes that 6 percent work for the federal government, 4 percent work in the motion picture and recording industries, and 3 percent work for personal care services.

Craft and fine artists had a median annual wage of $52,910 in 2023, according to the BLS. Half of craft and fine artists earned more than this amount, and half earned less. This is higher than the median annual wage for all occupations of $48,060. Fine artists, including painters, sculptors, and illustrators, have a higher median wage than craft artists. The BLS reports that fine artists have a median wage of $59,300, and craft artists have a median wage of $36,600.

The amount of income a craft or fine artist earns often depends on experience and reputation. Those just starting out earn less while they build their business, and those with a solid reputation earn more. The highest-paid craft and fine artists earned more than $129,440 annually, the BLS notes, while the lowest-paid earned less than $27,110 a year.

Happiness Is Being in the Studio

"Ultimately, I just find great enjoyment in making, and I try to imbue that into the objects I design, so others can share that enjoyment. This all circles back to my studio. If it wasn't a pleasurable place to be, I would not be doing what I'm doing. My hope is that what I make in my space inspires someone else to make something of their own."

—Eric Meyer, woodworker

Quoted in *American Craft*, "In My Studio: Eric Meyer," May 30, 2024. www.craftcouncil.org.

Future Outlook

The BLS expects demand for fine and craft artists to grow 4 percent by 2032, with about 5,500 job openings each year. Some of the demand for the works produced by craft and fine artists is driven by the economy because people are usually more interested in buying art when the economy is thriving. In a depressed economy, not as many people look to buy luxuries like art. Artists also face competition from machine-made goods that resemble handmade items, but an interest in locally made goods can offset this, the BLS notes. Private collectors and museums are also reliable buyers of artwork.

Find Out More

American Craft Council

www.craftcouncil.org

This website for the American Craft Council features information for artists who create handmade items. The Magazine section profiles craft artists, and the Events section lists craft shows taking place throughout the United States. Interviews with artists are featured in the American Craft Podcast section.

Art & Object

www.artandobject.com

This website offers news and videos about art shows being presented in museums and galleries around the world. Articles offer insights into contemporary art, Latin American art, Black artists, drawing, painting, and other topics. A search for "art schools" brings up articles ranking the top art schools in the United States.

New York Foundation for the Arts

www.nyfa.org

The Programs & Resources section of the website of the New York Foundation for the Arts offers articles and information of interest to artists. The "Professional Development" page offers online learning opportunities, including on-demand courses and workshops. Articles about entrepreneurship, careers, insurance, and finance are found in the Business of Art area.

Dancer

What Does a Dancer Do?

Dancer Destiny Wimpye, a member of the Pacific Northwest Ballet, thrives in front of an audience. She has had leading roles in *Swan Lake*, *Beauty and the Beast*, and George Balanchine's *The Nutcracker*. Her dance career has included performances at the White House and in a Mariah Carey holiday special. "The most rewarding part of being a dancer is being able to finally get on stage and just dance," she says. "I enjoy the rehearsal process, but there's no feeling like being able to share what you love with the audience."[27]

Tilly Evans-Krueger dances in musicals on Broadway, appearing in shows such as *The Outsiders* and *Moulin Rouge!* Her job is not easy, but it is fulfilling. "The workload within this industry can be exhausting," she says. "At the same time, when you're performing as part of a show that you really believe in, night after night, it feels like it's for a reason and a purpose. When a show sits right within your soul, even the hardest workdays are beyond worth it."[28]

Dancers perform onstage, showcasing their skill in ballet, hip hop, tap, jazz, or another dance style. Their performances may be

A Few Facts

Typical Earnings
$24.95 hourly wage in 2023

Educational Requirements
Formal dance training

Personal Qualities
Athletic ability and physical stamina, creativity, persistence, ability to work as part of a team, leadership skills

Work Settings
Dance studio, theater

Future Outlook
Growth rate of 5 percent through 2032

presented before a live audience or recorded for broadcast or video. Hayoung Roh has been a backup dancer for Kylie Minogue, danced in a show at a resort in Macau, and been part of dance companies in New York City. As a member of the Brooklynettes, she performs in front of fans at Brooklyn Nets basketball games.

The Workday

When ballerina Brittany Haws was performing, her days stretched from 7:00 a.m. to 11:00 p.m. After a light breakfast of fruit and porridge drizzled with honey, she headed to the theater. She liked to get there forty-five minutes to an hour before the 9:00 a.m. ballet class so she could stretch and warm up. The class included work at the barre, pirouettes, large jumps, and leaps.

The class ended at 10:15 a.m. and rehearsal began at 10:30 a.m., giving her just enough time to change into a fresh leotard. Rehearsals lasted until 1:00 p.m., and then she would head home for lunch. "I'd eat something that would give me energy without feeling overly full, and attempt to relax and rejuvenate before the evening performance," Haws says. "Sometimes, I even lay down to have a sneaky nap."[29]

She would have a banana or energy bar before heading for the theater about 3:45 p.m. After arriving, she would put on a makeup base and go to the dance studio for a thirty-minute warm-up class for dancers that began at 5:00 p.m. During this time Haws calmed her nerves and prepared mentally for the performance. She then did her makeup, had her hair done by a stylist, and got into her costume. Performances began at 6:30 p.m. and ended at 9:00 p.m. "There was often a sense of accomplishment for what I had achieved, although there was always room for improvement,"[30] she notes. After the performance, she showered, changed into regular clothes, and headed home. She would have supper and watch TV or a movie with her husband before heading to bed at about 11:00 p.m.

> ### Learning to Lead
>
> "I try to both give myself grace and hold myself accountable. In this role, it's important to develop one-on-one relationships with the dancers. I'm even taking a leadership coaching course, in order to consistently show up as my best self and help lead this group of amazing women."
>
> —Hayoung Roh, co-captain of the Brooklynettes, official dance team for the Brooklyn Nets basketball team
>
> Olivia Mannon, "Step Onto the Court with Brooklynettes Co-captain Hayoung Roh," *Dance Magazine*, May 22, 2024. www.dancemagazine.com.

Not every day is a performance day for professional dancers. Other days are filled with rehearsals, auditions, workouts, and dance classes. Regardless of whether there is a performance on the horizon, there is always something to rehearse and practice, Haws points out.

Haws and her husband have two children, and she is now a dance teacher. Teaching is also a big part of dancer Bella Klassen's day. She gets up at 6:00 a.m. and heads to the gym for a workout. At 9:00 a.m. she teaches a private dance lesson online. She takes dance classes from noon to 4:30 p.m. and then returns to teaching in the evening, helping young dancers improve.

Education and Training

Dancing requires dexterity, a sense of rhythm, and physical stamina, and it takes years for dancers to perfect their technique. They need formal training and may start taking lessons as young as age two or three. Classes are held after school, and dancers can attend camps and intensive programs during the summer. Dancers may relocate to a different part of the country to attend classes that fit their style and skill level. Wimpye moved from

Atlanta, Georgia, to Los Angeles at age nine to train at the Debbie Allen Dance Academy. At age thirteen she enrolled in the Colburn School, which offers rigorous training for teens who want to be professional dancers. "I think that helped me to mature, both mentally and emotionally," she says. "I gained the independence and strength that I need to succeed in this industry."[31]

It is possible to have a dance career without having formal training early on. Kyle Hanagami fell in love with dance after auditioning for the hip hop team at the University of California, Berkeley, as a freshman. He was an economics and psychology major, but his dance career took off after he posted videos of his moves on YouTube and began getting requests to teach dance all over the world. He danced for the Black Eyed Peas before turning his attention to choreography and working with stars like Ariana Grande, Jennifer Lopez, and Alicia Keys.

Some dancers begin their professional career immediately after high school, while others pursue a college degree. Evans-Krueger graduated from Wright State University with a bachelor of fine arts degree in dance. Roh got a bachelor of fine arts degree at New York University's Tisch School of the Arts, where she had classes in anatomy and music theory in addition to learning about many types of dance. She says the classes "helped me to become a well-rounded artist. It set me up for success."[32]

A college dance program may be part of its theater or fine arts department. Dancers who attend college may study a variety of styles, including jazz, hip hop, ballet, and modern dance.

Skills and Personality

Dancers need to be strong and limber to execute physically demanding movements, and they must have the endurance to last through lengthy rehearsals and performances. Beyond strength and stamina, though, dancers need to be creative, understand-

Dancers attend a final rehearsal before a performance. Before they ever set foot on a stage, dancers spend countless hours training, practicing, and rehearsing.

ing how to use movement to express ideas and emotions. They also need the mental and physical persistence to practice moves repeatedly to make them crisp and clean.

Persistence is also needed when auditioning for roles. "There are thousands of talented dancers, each wanting the same thing— a contract in a company," Haws says. "I did countless auditions, and they didn't always go to plan. Sometimes they're looking for a particular physique, only men, only women, only people with experience. It's difficult and tiring."[33]

Teamwork and interpersonal skills are also required because most dance classes are in a group setting, and dancers often perform in an ensemble. As they mature, dancers may take on leadership roles in which they teach, mentor, and support other dancers.

Working Conditions

Dancers rehearse in a studio and perform in theaters and arenas. They may be part of a musical on Broadway or perform with the

Dancing Is Her Superpower

"Even during the darkest times, I would go into the studio, turn some music on, and return to the real reason why I danced. I would tap into that 'aliveness' that fills my heart and soul, and it always gave me fuel to continue . . . as I get older, and the demands on my body through my career have changed how I can dance, I still know why I do it. I do it for the energy that comes alive in my body that doesn't show up any other time. Filling every cell with pure electricity and allowing me to bask in sensation while everything else melts away. It's like a secret superpower."

—Stacey Tookey, choreographer and professional dancer

Stacey Tookey, "Choreographer Stacey Tookey Shares How Dance Makes Her Feel Alive," *Dance Magazine*, April 17, 2024. www.dancemagazine.com.

New York City Ballet. Rather than working with a dance company that performs in one city, they could tour with a show and perform in theaters or stadiums all over the country. They may also be part of a musical revue on a cruise ship or at a theme park or resort.

Many jobs for dancers are in cities with strong art cultures, such as Los Angeles, New York, and San Fransisco. Las Vegas, Honolulu, and the Riverside/San Bernardino/Ontario area in California are also urban areas with many employment opportunities for dancers, according to the Bureau of Labor Statistics (BLS).

Employers and Earnings

Dancers audition for a part in a show, such as a Broadway musical, or a job with a dance company, such as the Alvin Ailey American Dance Theater in New York City or the Joffrey Ballet. Auditions are often a continuous part of a dancer's career, since a job ends when a show closes.

The median hourly wage for dancers was $24.95 in May 2023 (half of dancers make more than this wage, and half make less). The highest-paid dancers earned more than $48 per hour, while the lowest-paid earned less than $14.15, according to the BLS. Dancers have an average salary of $48,234 per year, according to Indeed, a career and job search website.

Dancers belonging to unions such as the Actors' Equity Association earn a minimum weekly salary established by the union that is based on the number of performances covered by a contract. They also receive health care benefits. Those on tour may receive a daily allowance to pay for lodging, meals, and other travel expenses.

Future Outlook

The BLS expects employment for dancers to grow by 5 percent through 2023. This is faster than the average growth of 3 percent for all occupations. Social media is expected to help increase the demand for dancers. The posts can reach a wide audience and get people excited about watching performances.

The BLS estimates that there will be 12,200 jobs for dancers in the United States by 2032. The number of new jobs for dancers may be tied to funding for the arts as well. If funding is tight, fewer shows will be produced and there will be less demand for dancers. If funding increases, demand could be greater.

Find Out More

Answers4Dancers

www.answers4dancers.com

This website offers job tips for dancers. It includes information about agencies, auditions, and pay. Members have access to additional information about auditions, dance jobs, and advice from professional dancers.

Dance Magazine

www.dancemagazine.com

Dance-related news and career information are featured on the website for *Dance Magazine*. The "College Guide" page contains information about dance programs at colleges and universities across the United States. The listings can be sorted by degree, location, and finances.

National Association of Schools of Dance

https://nasd.arts-accredit.org

This organization sets standards for dance and dance-related programs. On its website, information about dance programs throughout the United States can be found using the Find Accredited Institutions link. A brief description of the program, a link to its website, and contact information is provided.

Art Therapist

What Does an Art Therapist Do?

When patients from a Detroit hospital's behavioral unit come to Aishwerya Iyer's art therapy sessions, they may not know what art therapy is. She is amazed to see the impact the therapy has as patients find relief and comfort in expressing themselves through the creative process. "I am humbled and encouraged when patients and staff share that they look forward to art therapy," she says. "It is also inspiring to witness the resilience of people, even while in the depths of suffering."[34]

Tuesdai Johnson's mission is to raise awareness of the healing effects of art therapy. "It is both exciting and fulfilling to introduce a new form of therapy and art materials to clients, as well as witness the healing that takes place,"[35] says Johnson, who has a bachelor's degree in psychology and a master's degree in art therapy and counseling.

Art therapists like Iyer and Johnson are mental health professionals who help people use artistic expression to cope with mental health challenges. They have training in art and psychological theory, and they use their knowledge to

A Few Facts

Typical Earnings
Median annual pay of $57,120 for recreational therapists in 2023

Educational Requirements
Master's degree

Personal Qualities
Interest in art, communication skills, compassion, leadership skills, listening skills, patience, creativity, resourcefulness

Work Settings
Office, clinic, community center, recreation center

Future Outlook
Growth rate of 4 percent through 2032

help people work through trauma, anxiety, depression, and other mental health difficulties. Art therapists may work with people who have autism, behavioral challenges, or dementia. They can help people who have experienced a violent or traumatic event or who have been injured in an accident.

Art therapy can be woven into many different types of therapy programs. Art therapist Nick Denson works as a military and family life counselor for the US Air Force, and he describes himself as a creative healer. Be Staub is an associate marriage and family therapist and has specialized training in art therapy. Self-taught artist Soma Vajpayee has a master's degree in art therapy and is a child therapist, working with family counseling services. She is also a creative therapist in a hospital psychiatric unit. "In my life as an artist, I discovered a sanctuary of healing within the realm of colors and forms," she says. "That's what I wanted to share with the world when I started the journey to become an art therapist."[36]

The Workday

Art therapists' days depend on where they work and their role in the organization. Art therapist ToniAnn Eisman is the assistant director of a residential program, working with people who live in a setting where they receive therapy. She sets the therapy schedule for staff and clients, oversees payroll, and creates treatment and discharge plans for clients. She meets with clients individually and in groups for therapy sessions and runs art therapy groups. After each session she documents what has transpired. "If you're working with clients, you're going to be writing clinical notes which look at the factual data of the session,"[37] she explains.

Art therapists also need to keep track of art materials and order new ones when necessary. "Any and all art mediums can be used in art therapy," Eisman points out. "Colored pencils, colored pens, gel pens, paints, clay, crayons, any sort of collage material. You name it, any sort of art medium can be used."[38]

> **Overcoming Stigmas and Stereotypes**
>
> "My most valuable experience has come from working directly with a community-based group home for boys aged 13–17 who are facing adversities, particularly those who have committed delinquent offenses or have been labeled as children in need of supervision. Engaging with these youth allowed me to see beyond the stigmas and stereotypes associated with their situations. It reinforced my commitment to advocacy and ensuring that every individual I work with has a voice that deserves to be heard, regardless of their circumstances. This experience highlighted the importance of approaching their challenges with sensitivity and understanding."
>
> —Dejah Chapple, art therapy graduate student
>
> Quoted in American Art Therapy Association, "Featured Member: Dejah Chapple," May 7, 2024. www.arttherapy.org.

Art therapist Edie Morris uses clay, paint, and other materials in her job at a hospital that provides care for patients who have had a stroke, spinal cord injury, or traumatic brain injury. Patients meet with her to cope with changes in their physical and mental abilities as well as to process a traumatic event related to their injury.

She begins her day by organizing the materials she will need for her sessions and placing them on a cart she takes to patients' rooms. When she is ready to go, she pushes her cart loaded with paintbrushes, paint, clay, and other items through hospital hallways. To communicate with patients who have difficulty speaking, Morris points to images on an art-specific communication board. She may also use adaptive tools when working with patients, such as a wheelchair accessible loom, adaptive pottery wheel, or custom easels for mouth painting and drawing.

Seated beside his mother, a young boy works with an art therapist. Art therapists are mental health professionals who help people use artistic expression to cope with an array of mental health challenges.

Her day also includes patient evaluations and documentation of her observations. At the end of the day, she cleans her materials and fires her patients' finished clay projects in a kiln. After work, she unwinds by creating beaded artwork.

Education and Training

Art therapists are required to have a master's or doctoral degree. Depending on the state they work in, they may need a license in art therapy or a related field, such as professional counseling. They take an exam to become certified as an art therapist. They may receive Registered Art Therapist or Registered Art Therapist-Board Certified credentials.

The first step to becoming an art therapist is to graduate from college with a bachelor's degree. College courses for students looking to become art therapists are typically related to art and psychology. Eisman got a degree in painting and completed a second major in psychology. She then got her master's degree in creative arts therapy. "Art therapy is a very specific field in and of itself," she notes. "If you choose to master in some sort of related profession you might want to master in clinical psychology or in social work."[39]

In graduate school, students take studio art classes, including drawing, painting, and sculpting, as well as courses related to counseling, psychology, human growth and development, and adolescent development. Students also spend supervised time with clients. During her first year of graduate school, Eisman worked under supervision two days a week and had classes three days a week. During her second year, she attended classes two days a week and worked in the field for three days a week as an intern.

Skills and Personality

Art therapists must be compassionate, since they work with patients and clients who are coping with mental health challenges or painful situations. Empathy and patience are also important qualities, and art therapists must be good listeners when providing support. They also need to be resourceful and creative when developing projects and working with clients.

Good communication skills are also required, as art therapists must explain activities and give instructions. They may need to speak in front of a group, so public speaking skills are helpful. Leadership skills are needed to motivate people to participate in activities.

Art therapists typically enjoy creating art, but Morris notes that an art therapist does not need exceptional artistic ability. "Art therapy is rooted in the creative process rather than the end product being 'good,'" she explains. "It's more important for me to be knowledgeable about a large range of art mediums and techniques and know which mediums are appropriate to use with patients based on their therapeutic goals."[40]

Work Settings

An art therapist could work in a variety of settings, depending on their job and the clients they are working with. The Bureau of Labor Statistics (BLS) classifies art therapists as recreational therapists. About four in ten recreational therapists work in hospitals, and 27 percent work in nursing and residential care facilities. In addition to working for health care employers, they may work for the government or social assistance programs. Art therapists could also work in a school, rehabilitation center, psychiatric facility, cancer treatment center, veteran's clinic, or senior center. An art therapist may work in private practice and see clients in a dedicated office.

Because art therapy can be used in so many situations and settings, art therapists have the opportunity to help a variety of people. Eisman notes that this could include students, hospital patients, incarcerated individuals, or couples in family therapy. "The wonderful thing about art therapy is you can work with absolutely any population that you choose," Eisman comments. "You can work with children or adolescents specifically, adults, older adults, members of the LGBTQ-plus community, individuals with developmental disabilities, the homeless, veterans. Anybody is somebody that you can absolutely do art therapy with if they are willing to."[41]

Art therapists work full time and may see patients in the evening or on weekends if necessary. An art therapist may have a solo practice or work with other professionals such as occupational therapists, social workers, physical therapists, and psychologists, as well as a doctor or nurse, as they help patients develop skills for managing depression or anxiety or work with physical limitations.

Employers and Earnings

Recreational therapists, including art therapists, had a median annual wage of $57,120 in May 2023, according to the BLS. Half of recreational therapists made more than this amount, and half

> ### Using Art to Cope with Trauma
>
> "When in high school, I enjoyed and excelled in psychology classes. I was delighted to find the art therapy profession that married both my interests of art and psychology. I have worked with many children, as well as children living in adult bodies, who were unable to express preverbal experiences or traumatic experiences for which they had no words or a true understanding of their past emotional experiences which were interfering with becoming their true essence. I have learned that art therapy not only helps to make sense of one's experiences, but offers catharsis by bringing long held unconscious material to the conscious level."
>
> —Julie Houck, art therapist
>
> Julie Houck, "My Journey," American Art Therapy Association, 2022. www.art therapy.org.

made less. This is more than the median annual wage for all occupations of $48,060. The highest-earning recreational therapists worked for the government, making more than $72,000 a year.

Future Outlook

The BLS expects employment of recreational therapists, including art therapists, to grow at about 4 percent each year, which is a little above the expected average growth of 3 percent for all occupations. It anticipates that there will be thirteen hundred job openings for recreational therapists each year, with many occurring when people retire or transfer to a different occupation.

While funding challenges could impact job openings for art therapists, the need for them could grow as the population ages and therapists are needed to help seniors remain active and independent. Art therapists could also be needed to fill jobs that support people who are struggling with mental illness or addiction.

Find Out More

American Art Therapy Association
https://arttherapy.org

The website of this nonprofit organization dedicated to the art therapy profession offers a look at what art therapy is and what art therapists do. In the Featured Members section, art therapists describe what drew them to the career. The Education & Practice section offers information about how to become an art therapist and provides tips on selecting an education program.

Art Therapy Credentials Board
www.actb.org

The Art Therapy Credentials Board offers certification and credentialing for art therapists. Its website explains what art therapy is and how to obtain credentials. The Frequently Asked Questions section offers information on what art therapy treats, who uses it, and what it involves.

Psychology.org
www.psychology.org

Information about degree programs and career paths relating to psychology are featured on this website. Admission requirements, costs, and pros and cons of the degree are examined. A state search function brings up salary information and links to local programs.

Psychology Today
www.psychologytoday.com

The *Psychology Today* website contains articles on popular topics related to psychology. A search for art therapy brings up articles relating to the topic. The article "What Is Art Therapy?" includes an overview of what it is, its history, how it is used, and how to become an art therapist. It also has links to scientific studies that look at the impact of art therapy.

Sound Engineering Technician

What Does a Sound Engineering Technician Do?

Ramon Lupercio captures the sounds that make a television news piece complete. It could be the roar of an airplane, the rush of a waterfall, or goats bleating as they graze in a field. He teams up with photojournalists for interviews with people on the street, holding a boom microphone to get their comments. "We're watching out for each other, especially when it's breaking news," he says. "If the camera person has to worry about the audio, that's going to take attention away from their shoot."[42]

A sound engineer's job may be physical as well as technical. When he is on tour with a band, audio engineer Alex Markides does everything from unpacking and setting up microphones to operating the sound equipment to picking up cables after the show.

Without sound engineering technicians, also called audio engineers, the show would not go on. In a theater, they operate equipment that creates sound effects and allows actors' voices to be projected. At concerts, they make sure audience members can hear all elements of the performance, from vocals to instruments. Sports

A Few Facts

Typical Earnings
Median annual pay of $59,430 in 2023

Educational Requirements
Associate's or bachelor's degree

Personal Qualities
Communication skills, good hand-eye coordination, problem-solving skills

Work Settings
Recording studio or on location

Future Outlook
Growth rate of 2 percent through 2032

fans rely on them when they listen to a broadcast, and moviegoers can thank them for capturing dialogue and sound effects. In addition, their job may include recording, mixing, and editing music.

The Workday

Sound engineers work for many different organizations, and their workday will vary depending on who their employer is and what they are assigned to do. Lupercio's day is driven by what is happening in the world. He goes where the news needs to be covered, whether that is near a waterfall in Yosemite National Park or on a city street. He prepares for assignments by talking to the camera person and producer about where he will be traveling and the type of clothes he will need. He also plans the equipment he will need for the shoot and checks to make sure everything is set up properly. "Every time we have a shoot, I get a little anxious, so I start asking myself questions. How many people? How many mics?" he says. "I want to make sure I go there and check everything before we do our shoot, because the last thing you want is to be troubleshooting something when you're doing an interview."[43]

Markides has long days when he is on tour with a band. The sound equipment is stored in large trunks, and before the show Markides helps unload the trunks from a trailer. He takes the equipment onstage and sets the microphones wherever they need to be placed, including inside the drum set. During the show he operates the sound-system controls and monitors the screens at the digital audio workstation. After the show, he helps the crew take everything down. He removes the microphones, folds up the microphone stands, and packs things away. He works with a crew to pick up the cables snaking under the floorboards. He stows the equipment in trunks and takes these to the trailer with the crew. Once all the equipment is in place, he makes sure it is secure. Then it is time to travel to the next location.

Education and Training

A sound engineering technician's job may require postsecondary education, but a position could be gained with a high school diploma and hands-on experience. An understanding of how to operate the technical equipment is critical. To gain this practical experience, a sound engineer may work for a high school or college audiovisual department.

Lupercio began his career as a union courier for a network news station and learned the job of audio engineer by asking questions, reading instructions, and getting hands-on experience with equipment. His advice to current students is to get formal training and become familiar with sound engineering equipment. "If I had to start again, I would look into a broadcasting school for audio and video," he says. "I would get a manual of the mixer to see how it works. At bare minimum, get a microphone, a recorder, a cheap mixer and any camera that takes audio."[44]

Some post–high school programs offering certification for sound engineering or audio engineering technicians can be completed in a year or less. Courses may include instruction in studio recordings and engineering, recording in the field, audio for gaming, and sound system design. A sound engineer might also have a bachelor's degree in a field related to sound engineering, such as music, theater, the performing arts, or communications technology.

A sound engineering technician may take an exam to be certified by an organization such as the Audio Engineering Society, Society for Broadcast Engineers, or the Audiovisual and Integrated Experience Association. The certification shows that the technician meets the organization's standards and has knowledge of the subject. Membership in the organizations offers the opportunity to learn about new technology at industry events and also provides networking and continuing education opportunities.

Relationships Build Opportunities

"My advice to anybody that's trying to get into the business is to try to establish relationships, establish communication with people that are in the business. Get as much knowledge as you can, try to find some internships, try to find people like myself . . . in the business. Once you get those relationships, those relationships will turn to opportunities. A lot of the big events, a lot of the special programs I've been part of . . . most of those events I got them because of relationships I had."

—Damien Harris, audio engineer and production manager

Quoted in NAMM, "Production Manager/FOH Engineer Damien Harris," 2024. www.namm.org.

A desire to continue to learn and understand sound technology is vital, since the technology used in the field is constantly being upgraded. Learning how to operate sound engineering equipment can also be a way to enhance another career. Travis Holcombe had been a disc jockey since high school; he took a three-month course to learn how to use a digital audio workstation to record, arrange, and mix music. "I've been into music for a really long time," he says. "I wanted to take a class so I could . . . express the ideas I wanted to express through music."[45]

Skills and Personality

Sound engineering technicians need to be creative and have good problem-solving skills, since they must figure out how to get the best sound for each production or event. They need to understand which microphone is best for recording outdoors on a windy day, for example, so the sound of the wind does not overshadow the voice of the person speaking. When problems arise or equipment fails, they need to come up with a solution.

Manual dexterity and hand-eye coordination are important because sound audio technicians must move sliders, levers, and knobs to make adjustments to the sound during a broadcast or performance. When working at a concert or another event, they may need to have the physical ability to set up and take down equipment.

It also helps to have an ear for what makes a song work, or what sounds good. A sound engineering technician working in a recording studio or at a concert needs to operate the equipment in a way that enhances the sounds of musicians and singers.

Computer skills are needed to run the equipment and edit recordings, and communication skills are also required. Sound technicians collaborate with others to set up equipment and create recordings. When working with artists and musicians in a recording studio, they may need to be tactful as they work through differences of opinion on what the finished product should sound like. "I would never walk into a place or present a mix and say it's my way or the highway. I'd definitely invite comments,"[46] says Guy Massey, a Grammy Award–winning audio engineer and producer.

Working Conditions

Sound technicians may work indoors at a television station, on a movie set, or in a recording studio. When filming on location, covering a news event, or working at a concert or another event, the job might take them outdoors.

Work hours for sound engineers will vary, depending on their role. Those working for a television news program must work when a story needs to be covered or the show is being presented, and this could involve working at any time of day. Doing the sound for a concert tour means being on the road, which involves travel as well as working before, during, and after the concerts. Sound engineers on a movie set may work on weekends or evenings to meet a filming deadline.

A sound engineering technician may work full time, like Lupercio, but sound engineering may be a part-time job. Kelly Klaus is a sound engineer as well as a guitarist. He mixes sound for events and is also a member of a tribute band. Knowing how his own band should sound helps him in his engineering work.

Employers and Earnings

The Bureau of Labor Statistics (BLS) reports that the median annual income for sound engineering technicians is $59,430. Half of sound technicians earn below this level, and half earn above it. Sound engineering technicians may also be paid by the hour, and the median hourly wage is $28.57. The top-paying industry for sound engineering technicians is the software publishing industry. It has an average annual salary of $128,470.

Most sound engineering technicians work in the motion picture and video industries or the sound recording industries. They may also work for performing arts and sporting events, radio and television stations, or colleges and universities. Jobs for sound engineering technicians are primarily located in California, New York, Florida, Maryland, and Tennessee.

Future Outlook

There are about 17,600 jobs for sound engineering technicians in the United States, according to the BLS. It expects the total number of jobs to dip slightly, to 17,400, by 2032. There will be job openings due to people retiring or moving to other occupations, but advances in technology may limit the number of people needed to operate sound systems.

Sound engineering technicians will continue to be needed in the motion picture and sound recording industries, to provide high-quality audio for movies, television shows, and music.

Preparation Brings Confidence

"I used to get really nervous before sessions. A certain amount of butterflies is good. But having a confidence of walking into a studio and . . . just knowing what you want to achieve after discussions with the producer or, if you're producing it, with the artist, of what you want to achieve, my anxiety around that is definitely lessened. I just feel confident in what I do know. It's taken a long time, I've been doing this for 25 years. You're always learning something."

—Guy Massey, Grammy Award–winning audio engineer and producer

Quoted in Kevin Paul, "Guy Massey—Engineer/Producer Podcast," *Sound on Sound*, March 2024. www.soundonsound.com.

Find Out More

Audio Engineering Society
https://aes2.org
The Audio Engineering Society is an international organization devoted to audio technology. Its website has a student section with information about scholarships, courses, events, and competitions. Articles about technical advances in audio engineering can be found in the publications section of the website.

Audiovisual and Integrated Experience Association
www.avixa.org
The website for the Audiovisual and Integrated Experience Association offers a look at standards, training, and certifications for audiovisual professionals. Its training programs include a general knowledge course that provides foundational training for audiovisual design, installation, and management. It also offers courses relating to technology used at live events.

Society of Broadcast Engineers

https://sbe.org

This website for the association supporting broadcast and multimedia technology professionals offers information about broadcast engineering jobs and careers. It provides webinars on technical topics and information about certification exams in several areas. High school and college students studying broadcast engineering or a related field can join the organization.

Sound on Sound

www.soundonsound.com

News about audio technology and reviews of the latest equipment are featured on the website of *Sound on Sound* magazine. The website's SOS Podcasts feature interviews with people working in music production. In the People section, engineers, recording artists, and others in the recording industry offer insights on topics relating to sound production.

Source Notes

Introduction: Where Can an Interest in the Arts Take You?

1. Quoted in NAMM, "Production Manager/FOH Engineer Damien Harris," 2024. www.namm.org.

Chapter One: Graphic Designer

2. Quoted in DaShawn Brown, "Get to Know Charlotte FC's Graphic Designer," WSOC-TV, April 1, 2024. www.wsoctv.com.
3. Quoted in Brianna Flavin, "Is Graphic Design a Good Career? What I Wish I Knew BEFORE Becoming a Graphic Designer," *Design Blog*, Rasmussen University, May 19, 2023. www.rasmussen.edu.
4. Quoted in Brianna Flavin, "What Can You Do with a Graphic Design Degree? Exploring Your Options," *Design Blog*, Rasmussen University, May 11, 2023. www.rasmussen.edu.
5. Jesse Nyberg, *My Daily Work Life as a Graphic Designer in Los Angeles*, YouTube, April 3, 2023. www.youtube.com/watch?v=s02kN4Vv5bY.
6. Quoted in Flavin, "Is Graphic Design a Good Career?"
7. Quoted in Flavin, "What Can You Do with a Graphic Design Degree?"
8. Quoted in Flavin, "Is Graphic Design a Good Career?"
9. Quoted in Flavin, "Is Graphic Design a Good Career?"
10. Quoted in Brown, "Get to Know Charlotte FC's Graphic Designer."

Chapter Two: Art Teacher

11. Kristina Brown, "Unglamorous Truths: A Celebration of All Art Teachers Do During the School Year," The Art of Education University, May 22, 2024. https://theartofeducation.edu.
12. Andrea Wlodarczyk, "What Does a Day in the Life of an Art Teacher Look Like?," The Art of Education University, April 22, 2022. https://theartofeducation.edu.

13. Katie Vander Velden, interview by the author, June 26, 2024.
14. Vander Velden, interview.
15. Wlodarczyk, "What Does a Day in the Life of an Art Teacher Look Like?"
16. Vander Velden, interview.
17. Katie Jarvis, *Want to Be an Art Teacher? 10 Realities You Must Know About*, YouTube, March 23, 2024. www.youtube.com/watch?v=qkTA516blW4.
18. Vander Velden, interview.
19. Vander Velden, interview.
20. Vander Velden, interview.

Chapter Three: Craft or Fine Artist

21. Quoted in *American Craft*, "The Queue: Cedric Mitchell," June 10, 2024. www.craftcouncil.org.
22. Quoted in *American Craft*, "In My Studio: Eric Meyer," May 30, 2024. www.craftcouncil.org.
23. Quoted in *American Craft*, "The Queue: Ger Xiong," May 27, 2024. www.craftcouncil.org.
24. Fran Failla, "A Day in the Life of an Artist," *Fran Failla Fine Art* (blog), February 22, 2023. www.franfailla.com.
25. Jess Engle, *A Typical Day in My Life as an Artist*, YouTube, November 17, 2023. www.youtube.com/watch?v=lsgLdoh2fcA.
26. Engle, "A Typical Day in My Life as an Artist."

Chapter Four: Dancer

27. Quoted in Gigi Berardi, "Meet Pacific Northwest Ballet's Destiny Wimpye," *Dance Magazine*, April 25, 2024. www.dancemagazine.com.
28. Quoted in Olivia Manno, "Broadway Dancer Tilly Evans-Krueger Seeks Authenticity Above All," *Dance Magazine*, March 21, 2024. www.dancemagazine.com.
29. Brittany Haws, "A Day in the Life of a Professional Ballerina," Brittany Haws personal website, December 12, 2023. www.brittanyhaws.com.
30. Haws, "A Day in the Life of a Professional Ballerina."
31. Quoted in Berardi, "Meet Pacific Northwest Ballet's Destiny Wimpye."

32. Quoted in Olivia Mannon, "Step Onto the Court with Brooklynettes Co-captain Hayoung Roh," *Dance Magazine*, May 22, 2024. www.dancemagazine.com.
33. Haws, "A Day in the Life of a Professional Ballerina."

Chapter Five: Art Therapist

34. Quoted in American Art Therapy Association, "Featured Member: Aishwerya Iyer," April 3, 2024. https://arttherapy.org.
35. Quoted in American Art Therapy Association, "Featured Member: Tuesdai Johnson," March 6, 2024. https://arttherapy.org.
36. Quoted in American Art Therapy Association, "Featured Member: Soma Vajpayee," May 7, 2024. https://arttherapy.org.
37. Quoted in Ocean County Library, *So You Want to Be an Art Therapist*, YouTube, February 16, 2022. www.youtube.com/watch?v=kB8viQPhE6w.
38. Quoted in Ocean County Library, "So You Want to Be an Art Therapist."
39. Quoted in Ocean County Library, "So You Want to Be an Art Therapist."
40. Quoted in Shirley Ryan Abilitylab, "Day-in-the-Life with Art Therapist Edie Morris," September 23, 2020. www.sralab.org.
41. Quoted in Ocean County Library, "So You Want to Be an Art Therapist."

Chapter Six: Sound Engineering Technician

42. Quoted in NBCU Academy, "How Audio Engineers Make Your Pieces Sing," October 3, 2023. https://nbcuacademy.com.
43. Quoted in NBCU Academy, "How Audio Engineers Make Your Pieces Sing."
44. Quoted in NBCU Academy, "How Audio Engineers Make Your Pieces Sing."
45. Quoted in Point Blank Music School, "Hear from PBMS Alumni, Travis Holcombe (KCRW)." www.pointblankmusicschool.com.
46. Quoted in Kevin Paul, "Guy Massey—Engineer/Producer Podcast," *Sound on Sound*, March 2024. www.soundonsound.com.

Interview with a Craft Artist

Susan Mikkelson is a Colorado-based artist who works with clay. She began creating one-of-a-kind pieces in 1988. She answered questions about her career by email.

Q: Why did you become an artist?
A: Art sort of found me when I wasn't looking, but I always loved the arts. I started pottery more as a hobby and just fell in love with every aspect of it. I was selling pottery to buy the equipment to set up a studio at my home. I gave myself a goal of five years to see if I could make a living at it and do it full time, and 35 years later I am still at it.

Q: How did you learn to work with clay?
A: I began working in clay at a small studio in California. After my husband, daughter and I moved back to Colorado, clay was still just a hobby I loved. I took a few classes at a community college, where I learned the different techniques such as raku, pit firing, and salt firing. I bought a potter's wheel and was able to begin making pottery both at home and in class. The classes also taught me the basics of glaze making (which took me a good 20 years to perfect), firing a kiln, and a sense of what I would need to set up my own studio.

Q: Describe a typical workday.
A: A typical workday for me usually starts first thing in the morning. I am outside in my backyard unloading and loading kilns, then downstairs to my studio where I throw, trim, wax, and glaze, depending on the day. Every day is a little different, which keeps it from being repetitive. I try to work about eight hours a day and weekends about four hours or so a day. It's nice to be able to set my own work hours.

Q: Where do your ideas for your pieces come from?
A: I am most inspired by the beauty in nature. The two types of glazes I use reflect in that. The blues represent the waters of oceans, lakes, etc., and the multicolored represents the mountains and plains. I also use a variety of leaves and incorporate recycled glass in many pieces.

Q: Your cups, bowls, and plates are functional as well as artistic. What made you decide to create these types of pieces?
A: I learned many techniques in pottery, including raku (my first kiln was a raku kiln) and salt firing. Although I loved experimenting with those, it ultimately made more sense for me to create pottery pieces that were not only beautiful pieces of art, but ones that were meant to be used. This way a bowl could rest in a stand for decoration and also be taken out of that stand for a dinner party.

Q: What is your favorite thing to make?
A: I don't really have a favorite thing to make. I do love it when I am not just filling orders and store shelves and get moments to just sit at the wheel and see what happens. That doesn't happen often enough as I am a one-woman business with so many responsibilities. I guess the most honored items I make are cremation urns. It's my way of giving back.

Q: What skills do you find valuable in this job?
A: The ability to think in the future has been very valuable. Each piece takes about one month to finish so I need to know what I will need a month ahead. Also, I would say a hard work ethic. I am working alone so I have to keep myself accountable.

Q: What do you like most about your job?
A: I love being my own boss. I get what I put into it, and it is amazing creating what I love for others to enjoy. Every day is so different, and I love what I do.

Q: What do you like least about your job?
A: Sometimes it can be a little lonely, but my dog keeps me company! At times filling orders can be boring because it can be repetitive, for example, to make mugs again and again. They are a top seller, so I push through. Just like any job, at times I'm not in the mood.

Q: What personal qualities do you find most valuable for this type of work?
A: Good people skills are a must! You have to deal with customers, gallery owners, etc. I wasn't always great at that, but I've learned how to be much more confident. Also don't be afraid of HARD work. My husband says I'm the hardest worker he's ever known.

Q: What advice do you have for students who might be interested in this career?
A: If you believe in yourself and are willing to work hard, you can do anything you want! Go for it!

Other Jobs If You Like the Arts

Actor
Agent for entertainers
Animator
Art director
Band director
Cake decorator
Choreographer
Commercial artist
Composer
Fashion designer
Film and video editor
Florist
Illustrator
Interior designer
Landscape architect
Makeup artist
Movie director
Multimedia artist
Museum exhibit curator
Musician
Music teacher
Painter
Photographer
Podcaster
Radio or television broadcaster
Sculptor
Singer
Social media content creator
Tattoo artist
Web designer

Editor's note: The online *Occupational Outlook Handbook* of the US Department of Labor's Bureau of Labor Statistics is an excellent source of information on jobs in hundreds of career fields, including many of those listed here. The *Occupational Outlook Handbook* may be accessed online at www.bls.gov/ooh.

Index

Note: Boldface page numbers indicate illustrations.

actors, job outlook, 5
American Art Therapy Association, 46
American Craft Council, 29
American Institute of Graphic Arts (AIGA), 14
Answers4Dancers, 37
art directors
    earnings, 5
    job description, 12
    job outlook, 13
Art & Object, 30
arts and design occupations, 5, 61
art teachers
    basic facts about, 15
    earnings, 20–21
    educational requirements, 17–18
    employers, 20
    information sources, 22
    job description, 15–17, **19**, 19–20
    job outlook, 21
    personal skills and qualities, 18–19
art therapists
    basic facts about, 39
    certification, 42, 46
    earnings, 44–45
    educational requirements, 42–43
    employers, 44
    information sources, 46
    job description, 39–42, **42**, 44
    job outlook, 45
    personal skills and qualities, 43–44
Art Therapy Credentials Board, 46
Audio Engineering Society, 53
Audiovisual and Integrated Experience Association, 53

Bacon, Anna, 11
Baguley, Dimpho, 8–9
Brown, Kristina, 15
Bureau of Labor Statistics (BLS) art therapists' classification, 44
earnings
    art directors, 5
    art teachers, 20–21
    art therapists, 44–45
    craft or fine artists, 28
    dancers, 37
    graphic designers, 12–13
    median, for arts and design occupations, 5
    sound engineering technicians, 52
job outlook
    actors, 5
    arts and design occupations, 5
    art teachers, 21
    art therapists, 45
    choreographers, 5
    craft or fine artists, 29
    dancers, 5, 37
    graphic designers, 13
    musicians and singers, 5
    sound engineering technicians, 52
Occupational Outlook Handbook, 61

certification
    art therapists, 42, 46
    sound engineering technicians, 49
Chapple, Dejah, 41
choreographers, job outlook, 5
Colquitt, Kieren, 9
craft or fine artists
    basic facts about, 23
    earnings, 28
    educational requirements, 25–27, 58
    employers, 59
    information sources, 29–30
    interview with, 58–60
    job description, 23–25, **26**, 58
    job outlook, 29

personal skills and qualities, 25, 29, 59, 60

Dance Magazine, 38
dancers
  basic facts about, 31
  earnings, 37
  educational requirements, 33–34
  employers, 36
  information source, 37–38
  job description, 31–33, **35**, 35–36
  job outlook, 5, 37
  personal skills and qualities, 34–35, 36
Denson, Nick, 40
Deva, Eddie, 8, 9
digital interface designers, 12, 13

earnings
  art directors, 5
  art teachers, 15, 20–21
  art therapists, 39, 44–45
  craft or fine artists, 23, 28
  dancers, 31, 37
  graphic designers, 7, 12–13
  median, for arts and design occupations, 5
  sound engineering technicians, 47, 52
educational requirements
  art teachers, 15, 17–18
  art therapists, 39, 42–43
  craft or fine artists, 23, 25–27, 58
  dancers, 31, 33–34
  graphic designers, 7, 9–10
  sound engineering technicians, 47, 49–50
Eisman, ToniAnn, 40, 42–43, 44
employers
  art teachers, 20
  art therapists, 44
  craft or fine artists, 59
  dancers, 36
  graphic designers, 12
  sound engineering technicians, 51, 52
employment, part-time or seasonal, 5, 52

Engle, Jess, 24–25, 28
Evans-Krueger, Tilly, 31, 34

Failla, Fran, 24, 25
Ferlo, Joseph, 4
fine artists. *See* craft or fine artists

Graphic Artists Guild, 14
graphic designers
  basic facts about, 7
  earnings, 12–13
  educational requirements, 9–10
  employers, 12
  information sources, 14
  job description, 7–9, **10**, 11–12
  job outlook, 13
  personal skills and qualities, 9, 10–11

Hanagami, Kyle, 34
Hansen, Tessa, 7, 12
Harris, Damien, 4, 50
Haws, Brittany, 32–33, 35
Hertz, Ishel, 15–16
Holcombe, Travis, 50
Houck, Julie, 45

Iyer, Aishwerya, 39

Jarvis, Katie, 16, 18
job descriptions
  art directors, 12
  art teachers, 15–17, **19**, 19–20
  art therapists, 39–42, **42**, 44
  craft or fine artists, 23–25, **26**, 58
  dancers, 31–33, **35**, 35–36
  graphic designers, 7–9, **10**, 11–12
  sound engineering technicians, 47–48, 51–52
job outlook
  actors, 5
  art directors, 13
  arts and design occupations, 5
  art teachers, 15, 21
  art therapists, 39, 45
  choreographers, 5
  craft or fine artists, 23, 29
  dancers, 5, 31, 37

digital interface designers, 13
graphic designers, 7, 13
musicians and singers, 5
sound engineering technicians, 47, 52
web designers, 13
Johnson, Tuesdai, 39

Klassen, Bella, 33
Klaus, Kelly, 52

Lewin, Amy, 8
LoGalbo, Hannah, 13
Lupercio, Ramon, 47, 48, 49

Markides, Alex, 47, 48
Massey, Guy, 51, 53
Meyer, Eric, 23, 28, 29
Mikkelson, Susan, 58–60
Minogue, Kylie, 32
Mitchell, Cedric, 23
Morris, Edie, 41–42, 43
musicians, job outlook, 5

National Art Education Association, 22
National Association of Schools of Dance, 38
National Gallery of Art, 22
New York Foundation for the Arts, 30
Nyberg, Jesse, 7, 8

Occupational Outlook Handbook (Bureau of Labor Statistics), 61

part-time employment, 5, 52
personal skills and qualities
  art teachers, 15, 18–19
  art therapists, 39, 43–44
  craft or fine artists, 23, 25, 29, 59, 60
  dancers, 31, 34–35, 36
  graphic designers, 7, 9, 10–11
  sound engineering technicians, 47, 50–51, 53
potters, 58–60
Psychology.org, 46
Psychology Today (website), 46

recreational therapists, 44–45

Roh, Hayoung, 32, 33, 34
Ruane, Gabe, 10

seasonal employment, 5
singers, job outlook for, 5
Society for Experiential Graphic Design (SEGD), 13, 14
Society of Broadcast Engineers, 54
sound engineering technicians
  basic facts about, 47
  certification, 49
  earnings, 52
  educational requirements, 49–50
  employers, 51, 52
  getting started as, 50
  information sources, 53–54
  job description, 47–48, 51–52
  job outlook, 52
  personal skills and qualities, 50–51, 53
Sound on Sound (website), 54
Staub, Be, 40
Steingart, Alysia, 10–11

Teach.org, 22
Tocci, Nicole, 25
Tookey, Stacey, 36
training. *See* educational requirements

user experience (UX) designers, 12
user interface (UI) designers, 12

Vajpayee, Soma, 40
Vander Velden, Katie
  on being teacher with and without own classroom, 19–20
  on breaks between semesters, 20
  on handling students' energy, 18
  least favorite aspect of being art teacher, 18–19
  reasons for becoming art teacher, 18
  typical workday of, 16–17
Vona Studios, 8

web designers, 12, 13
Wimpye, Destiny, 31, 33–34
Wlodarczyk, Andrea, 16, 17, 21

Xiong, Ger, 23–24, 25